Osho's opportunism

Table of content

Preface,

osho's opportunism. osho was an opportunist. He used to present the facts in his own way to prove his point. I will put these facts before you, you have to decide.

osho read many books. Studied many philoshophers. it's a good thing. But did not know how to separate. Made Khichdi by mixing all of them. There are many routes to reach a place. But we will choose only one path. Can't walk on many routes simultaneously. Let's take another example, if I want to go to the other side of the river, I will sit in only one boat and not in many. Although all the boats will go to that side only. But osho chose many routes at once, tried to sit on many boats at once. And that's why he got this mood. That's why he acquired a lot of knowledge but could not imbibe the knowledge.

You say suppression is wrong and till now all the Vedas, Puranas and sages have shown suppression. While the reality is that they have taught to restrain the senses rather than suppression. There must be restraint on the senses because the senses do not have intelligence. That's why it cannot differentiate between good and bad. That's why senses should be curbed towards bad things, there is no suppression anywhere. Suppression means to suppress completely in every situation. osho has misrepresented the principles of Sanatana Dharma to establish his theory. osho was influenced by western civilization. He used to talk about Freud. But could not understand Freud's basic ideas.

Writing this book of mine will be successful if you imbibe this one sentence said by me. You become the master of your mind, not a slave. Make yourself in such a way that no one can change your mood by throwing a stone in your mind like a pond. If this happens, then it should be understood that you are making good progress on the yogic path. Following this is also beneficial for the general public. If you are not able to do this, then this fight is not with anyone else but with yourself. Because you have to get the first victory over yourself.

Osho's first lecture

Krishna's personality is very unique. The first point of uniqueness is that Krishna was in the past but is of the future. Man has still not been able to understand Krishna. It is still beyond human understanding. In future also it will not be possible that we can understand Krishna. There are some reasons for this, the biggest reason is that Krishna is the only person who is not serious, not sad, not crying while being in the ultimate depths and heights of religion. Generally, the sign of a saint should be crying, sad with life, lost and running away. Krishna is the only person dancing, laughing and singing. All the religions of the past were sadistic. Except Krishna, all the religions of the past were sad, full of tears. The smiling religion, the religion which accepts life in totality is yet to be born. Certainly the old religion and the old God which we used to consider as God, which was our concept of God, that too has died. It is said about Jesus that he never laughed. Perhaps this sad personality of Jesus, his body hanging on the cross itself became the reason of attraction for us sad minded people. Mahavir or Buddha were against this life in a very deep sense. There is some other life, there is some salvation in the hereafter, it is biased. Religions had divided life into two parts, one which is acceptable and the other which is unacceptable. Krishna alone accepts the whole of life. Acceptance of the totality of life resulted in his personality. That's why all other incarnations in this country are called partial incarnations. Krishna is called the complete incarnation. Ram is also a part of God. But Krishna is completely divine. And this is also the reason for thinking and understanding for saying this and that reason is that Krishna has imbibed everything. Krishna is a small island dancing alone in the ocean of sorrow. Or so we understand that there is a dancing little desert in the big desert of sadness, prohibition, condemnation and repression. They could not affect our entire life stream. We were not worthy that we could not imbibe them. Till now the mind of man kept thinking by breaking and thinking by duality. The body has to be rejected and the soul has to be accepted. So the soul and the body have to fight. The hereafter has to be accepted and this world has to be denied. And this world and the hereafter have to fight. Naturally, if we deny the body, the mind will become sad. Because all the blood sources of life, sensations, all health, music is coming from the body. The religion which denies the body will become yellow. The blood will become empty and redness will disappear from it. That religion will be dry like a yellow leaf. The belief of that religion which is deeply seated in the mind is also engaged in preparing to fall like a yellow leaf. Krishna is the only one who accepts the body in its totality i.e. its Totality. It is accepted not in one dimension but in all dimensions by Krishna in totality. Except perhaps Krishna, in the entire history of mankind till Europe, children are born crying. Only Krishna was born laughing. And Krishna accepts only humanity while laughing. The world of religion before Freud cannot exist after Freud. A great revolution has taken place and a great rift has occurred in the human consciousness. We can never reach where we were before Freud. A new peak has been touched and a new understanding has arisen in the human consciousness. Old religion used to teach suppression and suppression. Lust, anger, greed, attachment all have to be suppressed and destroyed. And only then there will be self-realization and God will be attained. This fight went on for a long time. In thousands of years of this fight there are only ten five people whom we can say have attained to God. In a sense this fight was not successful because billions of people died without finding God. There must have been some basic mistake, it is like a gardener planting 50,000 plants and one plant flowers and still following the scriptures of that gardener and we say, look, this plant has flowered. And forget this thing, if only one plant flowers out of fifty thousand plants, then it is not because of the gardener, but it must have somehow escaped from the gardener, that's why this plant flowered. Because the gardener's command is on the other fifty thousand plants as well, in which flowers do not grow, leaves do not come, they remain only stubble. If a Buddha, a Mahavira, a Christ become available to God despite conflicting religions, then this is not a proof of the success of any of the religions. The success of religions will be considered then, the gardener will be considered successful only when flowers come out of 50,000 out of 50,000 leaving only one and a half, then it will be understood that a plant which does not flower, it will not be the fault of the gardener, definitely the plant There must be some mistake in me. With Freud, this new consciousness was born that repression is wrong, and repression puts man into self-violence. If a man starts fighting with himself, he can only be destroyed. If I fight my left and right hand, neither the left will win nor the right will win, but I will be defeated. So repression made a man suicidal, he destroyed himself with his own hands. For the consciousness that was born after Krishna Freud, which understood, Krishna alone seems to be meaningful. Because Krishna is the only person in the history of old humanity who is not oppressive. He has accepted all the colors of life. They don't run away from love, they don't run away from men and women. They do not turn away from war while experiencing God. He is full of compassion and love and yet has the power to fight in battle with a non-violent mind.

Because where is the melody, where is the ash and where is the battlefield, there is no coordination between them. That's why I have caught each and every gross of Krishna, sorted out the one whom I fell in love with. He refused the rest of the gross. Gandhi called Geeta as mother but could not imbibe Geeta. Because where will Gandhi's non-violence keep the possibilities of war. So Gandhi finds a solution, he says that this war is just a metaphor, it never happened. This is the battle of good and evil within man. This Kurukshetra is not an external battlefield and it is not as if Krishna had fought Arjuna in an external war. This is an allegory of the war within. This is a story. This is a symbol. Gandhi has difficulty because if Gandhi has a mind, Arjun will be right. Great non-violence has arisen in Arjun's mind. He is ready to leave the war and run away. He says what is the use of killing loved ones. He says what will I do after getting money and fame by doing so much violence. It is better that I leave everything and become a beggar. It is better that I run away, bear all the sorrows. This makes my heart tremble a lot. So much violence is ominous. How can the words of Krishna be caught by Gandhi? Because Krishna explains to him that you fight. And the arguments they give for fighting are so unique that they have never been given before. Only the most non-violent can give him. Krishna's logic is that as long as you believe that you can kill, you are not a soulist. Till then you don't even know what is inside, it has never died and can never die. If you think that I will be able to kill, then you are in great delusion because the concept of killing is the concept of a materialist. No one dies for the one who knows this, Krishna says that dying and killing is an act, it is a play, it is a play. In this context, it would be appropriate to understand that we call the life of Ram a character. Ram is very serious. His life is not his character but his character. But Krishna is not serious, it is not Krishna's character, it is Krishna's leela. Ram is a person bound by limits. They will not move even a step beyond the limits. They will sacrifice everything on the limits. Krishna is completely independent. Who has no limit, who can go anywhere. There is no such place where he stayed. There is no limit where he gets scared and stops his step. This unlimitedness is also the ultimate result of Krishna's self-realization. So violence has also become dishonest there because violence cannot happen. And where violence becomes dishonest, non-violence also becomes dishonest. Because as long as violence is meaningful and violence can happen, non-violence is also meaningful. The real violent self is materialism. And to believe in non-violence is also the other end of the same materialism. One believes that I will kill, and the other says that I will not kill. But both believe that they can be killed. Such a spirituality that considers even war as a game. And who accepts all the directions of attachment, love, enjoyment, work, yoga, meditation together in all the directions of life. The possibility of understanding this is increasing every day. Because now we have come to know some things which we never knew before. But you must have known Krishna for sure. As we have come to know today that there are no two things like body and soul. The part of the soul which is visible is the body and the part which is not visible is the soul. There are no two things like God and the world. There is no conflict like God and nature anywhere. The part of God which has become visible is Prakriti and the part of Prakriti which has become invisible is Paramatma. There is no such place anywhere where nature ends and God begins. Prakriti itself becomes divine by being engrossed. It is God who becomes manifest and becomes Prakriti. This is the meaning of Advaita. And this Advaita that if the concept becomes clear to us, then the earth can be understood. Along with this, the value and significance of Krishna is going to increase in the future and why Krishna will come closer to human beings. Now suppression will not be possible. After a long struggle and search for knowledge, it has been known that the forces with which we fight are our own. That's why nothing can be more insane than fighting them. And it has also been known that we can never transform the one we fight with.

If a person fights with sex, celibacy will never happen in his life. If brahmacharya can happen, the only way is to transform the energy of his sex. Do not fight with the energy of sex, but cooperate with the energy of sex. Do not take enmity with the energy of sex, but make friendship with the energy of sex. Because we can change only those with whom we are friends. There is no question of changing the one with whom you have become an enemy. There is no way to understand the one whose enemy we are. We can understand only those with whom we have friendship. So what appears to us as the lowest is also the other end of the highest. The peak of the mountain and the gap under the mountain are not two events, they are two parts of the same event. The gap that has been made is made by the high rise of the mountain. This mountain has been able to rise up, it has been formed because of the formation of this gap. These are not two things, mountain and ditch are two in our language, there are two ends of one thing in existence. The tree that wants to touch the height of the sky has to reach its roots to the underworld. And if a tree is afraid of reaching its roots to the underworld, it has to give up its aspiration to reach the sky. In fact, the higher the height, the deeper one has to descend. The higher you want to go, the lower you have to go. Height and height are not two things, they are two dimensions of the same thing. And they are always the same, grow in the same proportion. Man's mind always wanted to make a choice, he wanted to save heaven and leave hell. He wanted to preserve the peace and release the tension. He wanted to save the good and leave the bad. He wanted light to remain light and not darkness. Man's mind breaks existence into two parts and chooses one part and rejects the other. Due to this duality was born. Krishna is the symbol of accepting both together. And one who accepts both together can be perfect. Otherwise, it will remain incomplete, as much as it chooses, that part will remain and the one it rejects, it will always be tied to it, it will not be able to go out of it. The person who suppresses the work, his mind will go on becoming sensual from free of work. That's why the culture that suppresses sex, that culture creates sexuality. If Krishna had been believed, then sensuality would have been separated from the world at this time. Don't know in how many ways we have denied those parts of Krishna in which there was acceptance of sex. But now it will be possible because now we have started to see that sex energy which is sex energy rises to the highest heights of brahmacharya. Life is not to run away from anyone, do not leave anyone in life. Life has to be lived by accepting it completely. The one who lives it in totality attains the perfection of life. That's why I say Krishna has a lot of value in the context of the future. And our present day brings us closer to that future where the image of Krishna will continue to flourish. And a laughing religion, a dancing religion will soon be created. And Krishna's stone will definitely be there in the foundations of that religion.

Question by a seeker

A huge Mahabharata war took place during the time of Krishna. And Krishna was in the main place in it and if he wanted, he could have stopped the war of Mahabharata. But this did not happen and a huge destruction took place and a huge responsibility for that destruction goes to Krishna. So was that a right thing or could Krishna be blamed.

Osho's answer (osho's lecture)

Same thing with regard to war and peace, then we want peace and no conflict, then we start elections and the world which is a meeting of dualities. And the world is the music of opposing voices. I have heard that a man used to play a musical instrument. And if he keeps playing the string for hours by keeping his hand at one place, then the people of the house will be worried and after that the people of the neighborhood will also get worried. Many people prayed to him that we have seen many instrument players, everyone's hand moves, everyone's different voices come out, what kind of melody have you taken. So the man said that he is still looking for the right place and I have found the right place. That's why I am staying at my right place. I don't need to search anymore. Our mind can choose only one tone of life. But there can be only one voice only in death. Life will stand on opposing voices only. The opposing bricks, standing against each other, hold the whole building together. Can anyone think that if the bricks are placed in only one direction then the building will collapse. The whole system of life is based on the tension of the opposing voices of life. War is also part of that tension. And war will harm us only, those who think like this, think incomplete, think wrong. If we go to understand the development of humanity, then we will come to know that the development of humanity has happened only through war. Whatever man has today, he primarily discovered in wars. If we see roads all over the earth today, they were made to send soldiers. They were not made to unite two men. They were not made to carry the wedding procession. Whatever means were there, if today we are seeing enlarged houses, earlier, not enlarged houses, but enlarged forts were built. And that war was needed. The first wall was built to fight against the enemy. Bankruptcy again, then houses touching the sky. Today we can't even imagine that there was a need for a war of houses touching the sky. All the resources that man has, all the prosperity, and all the scientific inventions have happened through war. In fact, war creates such a situation, it creates such an atmosphere of tension. The sleeping powers within us have to be awakened. We can be in laziness in the rod of peace, we can be in tamas. The sleeping powers within us have to rise on the occasion of challenge. So we don't remain ordinary in the stick of war. We become extraordinary. Man's brain starts working with its full power. And in war, a leap is made of man's talent. Which does not take place even in hundreds of years in the era of peace. Many people think that if Krishna had stopped the Mahabharata war, India would have been very prosperous. Then India would have touched the great pinnacle of development. But the thing is somewhat opposite, if we had met ten five more people like Krishna in the history of India and we would have fought not one but ten five Mahabharats, then today we would have been on the peak of development. Approximately five thousand years have passed since the time of Mahabharata. We did not fight any big war in five thousand years. The rest of our battles are very bankrupt. The rest of our fights have no value, they are petty fights. It would not be appropriate to call them war. If there is loss due to war, there is destruction, then we should be the most prosperous and developed on the earth. But the situation is opposite, the countries which have fought wars are very developed and prosperous. After the First World War, everyone used to think that Germany would break up forever. But the opposite happened, within just twenty years, Germany emerged many times more powerful. No one could have imagined that after the first world war, Germany would be able to wage the second world war. The intensity to which the First World War had brought his powers. He used that intensity. In the last second world war, it seemed that it would be very difficult to have a war now. And the two countries which were wiped out the most, Germany and Japan, both those countries stood up prosperous again. Looking at Japan today, one can say that the atom bomb was dropped on this country. Looking at India, it can definitely be said that atom bombs must have been falling here.

Looking at our plight, it seems that there have been wars going on here. This condition of India did not happen due to the war of Mahabharata. All the teachers who were born in India under the shadow of Mahabharata were anti-war. And they exploited the Mahabharata. No, now there is no need to fight. Now there is no need to fight. We could have touched the height of Mahabharata, the wave that our country's consciousness had touched, every time we could touch that wave of height. And perhaps today we would be the most prosperous and developed society on earth. This is also like thinking that war like Mahabharata does not happen in different societies. It is necessary to be prosperous even for the occurrence of war. And for prosperity also the occurrence of war is necessary. Actually they are challenge rods. If we had fought continuously in the war in which Krishna had brought us down because we thought about it, today we have almost reached where we were in the war of Mahabharata. Today, we have almost reached the same as it is a matter of weapons. Almost all the weapons available today were used in the Mahabharata. He was a very talented and scientifically advanced peak. There was no harm in that war. The moment of despair that gripped us after that war, that despair was misused. Some of the West has also caught hold of that pessimism rod. The West is also scared. And if there will be a downfall in the West, it will be because of the pacifists. If the West listens to the pacifists, the West will degenerate. He will reach the same place as we reached after Mahabharata. India accepted the words of the pacifist, that's why it took a long journey of five thousand years. It is necessary to think a little, Krishna is not a war fighter, but considers war also a part of the game of life. He is not a war eater, he has no ambition to destroy anyone, he has no thought of hurting anyone. He had taken all the measures to avoid war. But at the cost of life and truth and dharma, there is a limit to saving anything after all. After all, we do not want to wage war so that there is no harm to life. But if life is being harmed because of no war. But if peace is being broken because of the absence of war, then the power of a decisive war is needed. So Krishna is not actually a war eater or a war fighter, but he is also not a war slayer who is afraid of war. Krishna says that if there is no war then it is okay but if there is to be a war then it is not right to run away. And if war has to happen and such a situation arises that war becomes inevitable for the welfare of man and for the benefit of man, this inevitable war should be accepted with joy. Then it is also not right to carry it like a burden. Because the one who goes to war like a burden, his defeat is sure. The one who goes to war only for protection, his defeat is also sure. Because the mind which is filled with the sense of protection is not able to show its capability in fighting and showing bravery. He then keeps on taking preventive measures and keeps on shrinking. So Krishna tells to make fighting a joy. There is no question of hurting others. But the tension in life should always be in proportion. Whether auspicious or inauspicious will result, it is not necessary that war will only result in inauspicious. Never fighting can result in inauspicious results. Now our country remained a slave for a thousand years. This was the result of the weakness of our fighting ability. For five thousand years we became humble and poor. This was the result of lack of bravery and fearlessness in our personality. The desired sense of expansion or expansion was the result of deficiency in it. So there is no loss due to Krishna. Krishna's chain was not born, we could not create another Krishna. That's why the loss happened. And after Krishna's war it was natural that pessimism prevailed, it always does. And explain to the pessimistic teacher that all this is in vain, and see how much damage has been done. And this voice sat in our mind. And the community which is afraid of death, is afraid of war, is afraid of living, we are also afraid of living. So we are neither living nor dying, there is a trisanku between us. Now my understanding is this, if the world accepts the words of Gandhi, Binova, then the world will be at a loss. There is no need to fear war. But the earth has become too small for war, this is definitely true. In fact, a place is also needed for war. The resources we have have become so big that now there can be no war on earth. Now war on earth is dishonorable.Now the face of war has changed. Now the expansion of the war will increase further. Now the war will be fought on the moon, stars, Mars, planets and satellites. Scientists estimate that there should be about 500 million planets on which there should be life. So the one who has become fearful today, don't make hydrogen bomb, don't make atom bomb, if the word of this fearful man is accepted, then the campaign that can be done on the expansion of this world. The journey that can happen will not happen. Now the earth has definitely reached the point where war is dishonest. But this has not happened because it is also a matter of understanding, war has become meaningless today, not because the point of pacifist has been understood. War has become meaningless because the science of war has been fully developed. Total war has developed. War has become so total that it has become completely dishonest to fight on earth because war will have meaning only if someone wins or loses. No one will win and no one will lose in the war that is going on now. In that both will die together. Now war has no meaning on earth. And I believe that because of this the earth will now become one, its condition is no more than that of a global village. It has become like a small village. Smaller than two villages. The time it took to cover two villages. Now it takes that much time to go round the whole earth. So the earth has become so small, now war on earth is dishonest. And if there is a war on earth, it would be a mindless thing. It does not mean that there will be no war, it does not mean that there will be no war. Wars will continue to happen. But now there will be new lands, there will be new journeys and campaigns. The war has not stopped even after so many persuasions. It cannot be stopped, it is a part of life. Now it is a matter of great interest that what has not been born from the war. If you look very carefully, the entire system of our cooperation was created for the war. Cooperation for conflict. All cooperation is for struggle. If there is no war on land, there will be no cooperation or cooperation. So it is necessary to understand Krishna, then Krishna is not a pacifist, nor a warist. Actually the meaning of argument is to choose one of the two. Krishna is avadi. Krishna says that if peace results in happiness then it is welcome and if war results in happiness then it is also welcome. Krishna says that the one who speeds up the journey to Mars, the one who develops religion, the one who increases the possibility of happiness in life, is welcome. Such a welcome is needed. If our country had understood Krishna, then our country would not have become impotent. Don't know how many ugliness we have hidden behind many good things. Our cowardice is hidden behind our talk of non-violence. Behind our opposition to war is hidden our fear of death. But the war doesn't stop because we don't fight. Knowing our war, someone continues the war on us. If we don't go to fight, the war will not stop, rather we will become slaves. And yet they are dragged into battles. Now it is a matter of great fun that we did not fight, someone dominated us and made us slaves. And then we keep fighting in his army. The fighting has not stopped. Sometimes we fought in the Mughal army and sometimes we fought in the British army. We didn't fight ourselves, we remained slaves and kept fighting to save our slavery. The fighting has not stopped. Yes, this much happened, we fought for our freedom, fought for our lives, then we fought for our subordination, so that our subordination remained, for this our men kept dying. This is a sad result. This did not happen because of Mahabharata, it happened because we could not dare to do another Mahabharata. That's why I say that it is a little difficult to understand Krishna. It is very easy to understand the words of a pacifist. It is very easy to understand the words of war-lovers also, because they say that war is life. It is difficult to understand Krishna's point because he says life passes through both the doors. It passes through peace and it also passes through war. And if you want to maintain peace, then you have to have the ability to fight. And if you want to continue the war, then you have to prepare for peace. These are two legs, if you cut any of them, you will become lame and crippled. Genghis, Timur also limped and Gandhi and Russell also limped. They have only one leg. There cannot be speed through this. And that's why if there is a man with only one leg, he cannot move. Krishna has both legs, he is not a lame man. When Genghis goes away after fighting like Hitler, talks about peace like Gandhi. And I agree that both should have each leg. Krishna is useful for the future. Because a crucial thing has to be decided in the future. That the whole world has to be made peaceful, then a kind of deadness will prevail. Which is not possible, no one will agree, no pacifist will continue to take out his procession and keep hoisting the flags of peace.No one accepts. The war eater will keep preparing for his war. Their influence remains for ten and twenty years, then their influence remains for ten and twenty years. Krishna's talk is about the whole life and if we understand this, then neither there is a need to give up peace nor there is a need to give up war. The ground of war will definitely change everyday because Krishna is not a Genghis Khan, he has no eagerness to kill anyone or hurt anyone. Now let us see how the conditions of war change. If man does not fight with man, then all men together will start fighting with nature. Now this is a matter to think about, in those countries where war continued, science developed in those countries, they have the ability to fight. They fight with man as well and if they get time, they fight with nature as well. But our community did not even fight with nature after

Mahabharata. Didn't fight with flood, didn't fight with storm, didn't fight with mountain, didn't fight with any element of nature, that's why science didn't develop. Man will keep fighting and discover the secrets of nature even from the ground. Tomorrow he will fight with the nature of moon and stars, his campaign will not stop. So keep in mind that the society which is immersed in the war, only that society can put its men on the moon and stars. We could not remove it, the peace activist could not remove it. And the moon will be very valuable in the context of war, if not today, because whoever has the moon in his hand will have the earth in his hand. Because in the coming era, whose missiles will be hit on the moon, the earth will be in his hands. Now the quarrel is removed from the earth. Keeping countries like Vietnam, Cambodia, India, Pakistan confused with each other, all this is a matter of confusing the mind of the mindless. The real battle has now begun on the second floor. Going to the moon has a deeper and different meaning. The real thing is that no one on earth can challenge the one who has the moon in his hand. His atom bomb and hydrogen bomb cannons will always be towards the earth. There is no need to fire cannons on each country, countries will automatically keep coming in front of missiles. Because the earth keeps on rotating, and all the countries keep coming in front of the moon, so there is no need to go to different countries and drop bombs.

That's why about one billion eighty million dollars have been spent to land a man on the moon. This was not a game. There were reasons for this. And who will take off first? This race is similar to that once, three hundred years ago, all the countries of Europe ran towards Asia. And the ships of all the countries of Europe had raced to Asia, Portuguese as well, Spanish as well, French as well, English as well. Three hundred years ago, as if it had become necessary to occupy the land of Asia, for the development of expansionists. Now he has become dishonest. The people of Asia think that our fight has made us free. There is only half truth in this. The second truth is that now there is no point in occupying the land of Asia. That race is over. Now the vision is somewhere else. Now there is a race. This is a campaign and those who get hold of the mortal in this campaign are slowly destroyed. We are such a destroyed community. And that's why Krishna's message is very meaningful not only for us, I believe that the West has also stood at the place where it will have to fight yet again a decisive battle on earth. Certainly not on earth. If there will be competition on Earth, it will be on the Moon or Mars. There is no point in fighting on earth because both will die if they fight on earth. That's why we have to go to some other planet and decide who wins. Perhaps the situation has become the same again as it was at the time of Mahabharata. Even at the time of Mahabharata, there were two classes, there was a class which was completely materialistic, they did not accept anything other than the body. Whose vision does not have equality of any yoga other than enjoyment. It was a matter of the existence of the soul or not. Life was only indulgence, plunder, khasoot. Life had no meaning outside the body and the senses. That struggle was against the same class. Krishna had to get that struggle done, it had become necessary. May the powers of auspiciousness not prove to be weak and impotent. Even today the situation is almost the same. And it will happen within about twenty years. On the one hand materialistic materialism will stand with its full force. And on the other hand, there will be weak forces of good. Shubh has a basic weakness, he wants to withdraw from fighting. Arjun is a good man. The word Arjuna means a simple man. A Riju means neither crooked nor crooked. Simple minded. Let's see who will bother unnecessarily. He says don't fight leave the world. Krishna Arjuna is more simple but not straightforward. There is no measure of Krishna's simplicity, but simplicity is not weakness. And simplicity is not an escape. They have stood firm, they will not let you run away. Perhaps then the earth will split into two parts and this has always happened. That decisive decisive movements come when it comes to fighting again. Gandhi and Russell will not be of use in this. Because in a sense they are all Arjuna. They will say move away, they will say die but don't fight. A personality like Krishna is needed again. Those who say that auspicious ones should also fight. Shubh should also keep a sword in his hand. Certainly, when auspicious takes a sword in his hand, no one is inauspicious. It cannot be inauspicious, because there is no battle to fight. But the inauspicious should not win, so we have to fight. So this world will be divided into two parts. One part will be materialistic and the other part will be for freedom, democracy, individual and other values of life. But can such a class of other auspicious get another Krishna. Because whenever the conditions of human beings come to such a place that the decisive event is about to happen. So our situation calls out to that consciousness, it also gives birth to that consciousness, that person is also born, that's why I say that Krishna has great importance for the future. And when the population of simple and straightforward people becomes dishonest because the bad man is neither afraid nor afraid of the voices of the good man. It goes on growing, but the more a good man shrinks, the more a bad man is in joy. After the Mahabharata, there were many good men in India. Buddha is Mahavir, there is no limit to his goodness. But the mind shrank due to the flow of his goodness. And on that shrunken mind the aggressors of the whole world broke down. Not only do we go to attack, we are the ones who call for the attack. And you are not only responsible when you kill someone, but you are also responsible when you get killed. Because when you slap a person, not only you are responsible, fifty percent is also responsible for the one who has invited, tolerated, accepted, called and said to slap. If someone slaps you, then you are also 50% responsible, you call. The long queue of good men shrunk the heart of this country and we invited them to come. Accepting our invitation, many people came, kept us silent for years, pressed us, harassed us. He also went away from his death. But still our mood is hesitant. If Mao enters this country, Mao alone will not be responsible for it. A person predicted that communism would reach London from Moscow via Beijing, Calcutta. His prediction seems to be very correct. Beijing has reached, its footsteps are being heard in Calcutta. London is not far away. Now there is no difficulty in entering Calcutta. Because the mind of India is shrunk and will be suppressed by accepting it.

Questioner - How to know who is auspicious and who is inauspicious?

osho's answer - Whenever there is a rod of such crisis, whenever there is a decision to be made as to who is auspicious and who is inauspicious, there is always a difficulty. It was not easy that day either. Because only Duryodhana was not there on that side. On that side Bhishma too, there were good people on that side too. And not only Krishna was not there, not only Arjuna was not on this side. There were bad people on this side too. It is always difficult to decide in the decisive rod. But the price determines something. What did Duryodhana fight for? Whether the man is good or bad with him is not so valuable. What was he fighting for? What were the values of his fighting. If Krishna was motivating Arjuna to fight then what was the value. One of the biggest deciding value was justice. What is justice? What was fair? So today again we have to decide what is fair.

Now in my understanding freedom is justice and dependence is injustice. The class which pushes man into some dependence. He is on the side of injustice. There can be good men on that side. Because it is not necessary that good people should also be visionary. Confused. They don't even know that what they are doing is on the side of evil. Freedom is a very touchy thing. We need such a society, such a world, by which the freedom of man increases. The thing which reduces freedom, such a society and world should not be needed. Naturally, those who want to bring about subordination, will also not use the word subservience, because anyone will be moved as soon as they hear its use. They will also find such words which have a sense of dependence, but the feeling of dependence does not come. There is such a new word and that is equality. This word is full of cleverness. And there are some people who plead for equality by cutting freedom to one side. They say equality is needed. He also says that without equality how would there be freedom. They say that the primary thing is equality and they also say that without equality how will there be freedom. And if ever liberty has to be cut to bring about equality, we will be ready. Now this is a very funny thing, equality has to be brought because freedom is needed and freedom has to be cut because equality is needed. And once freedom is lost it is very impossible to get it, who will get it. I say you will have to fetter people to make them equal. Because without chaining someone's head is big, someone's leg is big, all of them cannot be cut. So, to make everyone equal, first they are chained, then we will make everyone equal by cutting off their hands and legs. But the one who makes everyone equal will remain unequal. He will stay away from you, he will not have chains in his hands but will have swords. And once there will be chains in your hands and swords in the hands of others and your hands and legs will have been cut then what will you do. Marcus had such a thought. Once to bring equality, freedom will have to be lost, individual freedom will have to be destroyed. A Dictatorship would be needed. Then when the work of equality is completed then freedom will be given. But the one who has so much power in his hand to do the same, he will give good freedom. Symptoms are not visible. Rather, the more a man's strength increases and on the other hand, the more a man becomes paralyzed, the more the matter of freedom ends because you cannot even ask, you cannot raise your voice, you cannot rebel. Freedom will be cut under the guise of equality. And freedom once cut is a difficult matter to return. Because when freedom is cut off, the reaper also cuts off the possibilities of future freedom. And secondly, freedom is a very natural thing that everyone should have. And equality is absolutely an uncomfortable thing that cannot be achieved. This is psychological, we are equating man, he cannot be equal, he is not equal. Man is fundamentally unequal. Freedom is definitely needed and so much freedom is needed that every person needs his full chance to be what he can be. So in my view Krishna's side is the side of freedom. There cannot be equality. If there is freedom then gradually inequality can be reduced. Keep in mind that I am saying that the sky can be reduced. I am not saying that equality can come. If there is freedom, inequality can gradually reduce. But if equality is imposed forcefully, then freedom gradually decreases. Forcefully imposed thing is synonymous with dependence. So the value has to be chosen. The one who is always inauspicious does not want to give value to the person. Because the individual is the element of rebellion. That's why the forces of evil believe in the group but do not believe in the person. It is very difficult to get wrong work done by an individual but it is easy to get it done by a group. It is not easy to get a single Hindu to set fire to a mosque, it is very easy to get a crowd of Hindus to set it on fire. It is difficult for a single Muslim to stab a Hindu child. But it is easy for a Muslim group to do the same thing. In fact, the bigger the crowd, the less the Self becomes. Because what is the essence of being is personal responsibility. When I stab you in the chest, my conscience tells me what I am doing. But when I walk with a crowd, then my conscience says that I am not doing it, people are doing it. And tomorrow I cannot be held personally responsible. The one who is inauspicious always attracts the group. The evil wants the individual to disappear and only the crowd remain. He wants an auspicious person, he wants the crowd to end but the person remains. Relationship will remain if individuals remain, but it will not be a crowd, it will be a society. Now it is also worth understanding that where there is an individual, there can be a society. And when the power of a person is less, there is only a crowd, there cannot be a society. This is the only difference between society and crowd. When I freely connect with you free person, a society is formed. There is no society in a jail, there is only a crowd. Prisoners are also related, laugh at each other and also send cigarettes and bidis to each other. But there is a crowd, there is no society. They are all gathered there not their choice of freedom. That's why the freedom of individuality, soul, religion and the possibility of the invisible and the unknown, whichever side prevails, is not confirmed even when Ram and Ravana fight because Ravana also has some Ram in him. And there is a little Ravan in Ram too. There are some Pandavas in Kauravas as well and there are some Kauravas in Pandavas too. There is not such a good man on earth who does not have a little bit of evil and there is not such a bad man who does not have some goodness. So it is always a question of proportion and strength. Freedom is the value of personality, soul, religion.

Osho's second lecture

A friend Hans Raj Bisnoi came, he asked many questions, from him you will come to know to what depth Indian stupidity has reached. It has entered even the soul. The first question they have asked is God you said you are God. God is omnipotent, omnipresent, omnipresent. Can you stop the rising of the sun for a few days or make any changes in the universe. Please tell In the second question, he has asked that God never dies, cannot die, it is impossible to die. Then why is there so much security in the ashram here? Why do we have to go through a metal detector? The third question has been asked that I can feel the desire of worship within you. Do you want people to worship you? If this is not an aspiration then why this picture has been put on your rosary. None of the questions asked by Hansraj Vishnoi is meaningful. But there are bound assumptions. Questions start arising from those bounded beliefs. But he is now trapped by asking. Will not be able to run away now. Hansraj Vishnoi how did you know that God is omnipotent, omnipresent, omnipresent. (Yogacharya Anmol - Exactly this is my question that how do you know that God is not omnipotent, omniscient and omnipresent and if you do not know then you also have no right to speak) We have met somewhere. You also know that there is God. Till date no one has been able to give proof and all the proofs that have been given can be refuted. Hansraj Vishnoi, if a little argument is needed, your stupidity has become less. (Yogacharya Anmol - Yes, you can't get God through logic, you didn't even know this much, God is a matter of faith, here I see you as a scoundrel, yes, you break your logic with logic and then I will also I will destroy you with arguments and this process is never going to end, what progress have you made in spirituality. It would have given a little wisdom, there is so much poverty in the world, more than half of the world is dying of hunger and you say that God is Almighty. (Yogacharya Anmol - Here everyone has the right to work, here every person is free to do work and on the basis of those deeds, a person suffers good or bad results, you write your own deeds and blame God, on your own You become knowledgeable, but even this much knowledge could not come within you, if someone is begging, then it is God's fault, the drenched person does not want to work hard and you are putting the fault on God) it means that he wants Be kind These drenched children on the streets, without getting milk. (Yogacharya Anmol - Beggar is not made by God, he himself has chosen that path, because he doesn't want to work hard, so he adopts shortcut method, you are talking like children as if you don't know these things) The widespread hunger, disease and poverty definitely gives proof of Almighty God. Awesome Almighty. Why are these lame children born? Why are these blind children born? Why are these children born with a rigid intellect? (Yogacharya Anmol - This is Karma Kshetra, today everyone has the right to work here, everyone can write their own luck, if you do bad deeds, then you will not suffer the consequences in this life, then you will suffer in the next life, you think that by doing bad deeds And if you are born lame then it will not be a surprise because you are also doing bad things, you are hurting the faith of crores of people, when the faith gets hurt, there is pain and there is someone who hurts. How can an act be right, while killing, raping, stealing, no one thinks but when the consequences are to be suffered in the next life, God remembers that God has done this. A person like you who knows this. If there is a soul, then the theory of Karma must also be known, and knowing all this, why are you asking questions like fools, yes you are asking these questions because you have to keep your point high and God down, high If you want to rise, then rise by yourself, you cannot rise high by making someone down, this is your opportunism, you make things fit according to your Maharaj)

Your Almighty God cannot do any good work even this much. Do you have the basis that God is omnipotent. And you are just saying that the matter is absolutely proven. There is no question of any doubt. There is no but but it is clearly declared that God is omnipotent, omnipresent, omnipresent. Well, if God is omnipresent, then the world must be of some other type. (Yogacharya Anmol - Whether the world will become good or bad is up to the human beings, the world writes its own destiny by its own actions) This world created by Sarvagya is not known. Why does Sarvagya make cancer, doesn't he have that much intelligence. Why causes tuberculosis? Sarvagya should have some intelligence. From whom nothing is hidden then all this hell that you are finding all around you. Whose handiwork is this, and you say that God is omnipresent. (Yogacharya Anmol - The actions of human beings only, because when a person does a good deed, he himself takes credit for it, but after doing bad deeds, when he is suffering the consequences, he blames God, why is God doing this to me? Is doing, brother, while doing bad deeds, did not remember God. You keep stuffing pizza, burger, rotten meat, things made in boiled oil like samosa, jalebi, all fast food in the stomach and these rotten things Don't look at your own handiwork, you are asking a donkey-like question to which everyone will answer. Don't know how he became a guru.) Hansraj Vishnoi has come from Haryana. Mandi Dabwali Haryana. Means there is a market in Haryana as well as in Dabwali. Then why have you come here? Would have met there. He is omnipresent, he would have met wherever he wanted. The discussion would have taken place wherever they wanted. (Yogacharya Anmol - Wow, the height of your pride is at its peak, it is clearly visible in your words) But we sit holding such things. Without thinking, without thinking, without searching. And we start blaming such things on others. I want to tell you clearly that I am not omnipotent. You are saying that can you stop the sun with some rods, I cannot even stop this electric fan. You ask can you make any change in the universe. What is your intention to bring about the change? The Almighty created this earth, the omnipresent created this nature, the omnipresent created this nature. If I do anything now, it will only spoil. There can be no improvement in this. Now what can be more universal than universal. And you ask whether God is neither dead nor can die. The first question is whether he ever lived. Had he lived, he would have died. How will you not die when you have lived? Born when Always talk from the beginning. Had he been born, he would have died. One thing is certain that he is not born. Jiya will not die, what will happen. Even if he wants to die, he cannot die. Gotta be there to die. First you have to prove that he was born, how he was born, with whom he was born. Who are the parents of your God? Only then will a long series begin. Then there will be their parents. Then there will be their parents. People consider such foolish thing as religious idea. And you are asking me this, but did you ask Krishna, Ram, Buddha, Mahavir about this? You call Krishna God whether Krishna died or not. (Yogacharya Anmol - Lord Krishna lifted the Govardhan mountain, can you lift it? Now don't say that Lord Krishna never existed because you have given all the above lecture on Lord Krishna only, so now you are denying his existence and pastimes. Can't, Lord Krishna had shown his universal form, can you show, let's go to become God, first you become a human being.) You call Buddha God whether Buddha died or not. You call Ram God whether Ram died or not. You want to make some different rules regarding me. I will die too And I don't see any harm in dying. You have to enjoy dying too. Living and dying are two sides of the same coin. But one interesting thing is that the process of the intellect of this country is very dual. If you raise the question of Ram then Ram is God. Then no one will ask how to die. And Krishna is God, how did he die? Buddha is God. Lord Mahavir. There is a lack of some gods here. All are dead, only one of them is still alive. Catch him if he is alive. (Yogacharya Anmol - God himself had left the body not that he had died, the body is left according to his wish, but in death man cannot leave his body according to his wish, many yogis have left their body according to their wish. What a big deal for God) and you ask why so much security arrangements here. Arrangement of security No one can stop my death. I will die. Security arrangements will also be there and I will die. Security arrangements are for some other reason. Even if I want to die, I want to die in my own way. I don't want to die from the hands of an idiot. I have my own way of life, I should have my own way of dying. I live with my pleasure and I will die with my pleasure. Krishna died after shooting an arrow in the leg of a man. Krishna was resting under a sleeping tree and a hunter shot him with an arrow by mistake. This is how death happened. Buddha died from food poisoning. A man fed the food and the food was poisoned. Mahavira died of dysentery. It should happen. This is going to be the result of one who fasts more. Stomach will be upset. (Yogacharya Anmol - Yes, it was Bali of Tretayuga who killed Lord Krishna. And it happened as per Lord Krishna's will. And secondly, even after burning Lord Krishna's body, his heart did not burn because he was an incarnation of Vishnu. Even today, Jagannath is in the temple. We all worship him. Wasn't your heart burning even after lighting it? You are becoming a god, do just one thing done by Lord Krishna, show it as a universal form, If not Govardhan mountain, then lift any small mountain. You will keep on saying empty words, I am God. Lord Ram was not dead. Even before Kaal came, Lord Ram was asked for permission. Because Lord Ram was Vishnu. Lord Ram opened the Saryu river I had attained samadhi by entering M. Instead of becoming God, if only you could have understood God that Lord Ram and Krishna are only God) I have at least this much right to die in my own way. And you ask this security if you are God then what is the need of security. Ram Chandra ji used to walk with bow and arrow. Is he going to Delhi to participate in Republic Day? That there will be a procession. What is he keeping the bow and arrows for? To drive away mosquitoes etc. To kill bedbugs. The questions you are asking me, first ask your Gods. Because first of all this Hansraj Vishnoi is not your God. What is your relation with me? You ask your Gods why you are roaming around with bow and arrow. Mind is bad. And the bow and arrow is clearly telling that the arrangement for security. And what was it when Krishna turned the wheel. If there was no security then what was it? Parshuram kept cutting people with his ax throughout his life and still you are considering him as God. Neither I have taken any bow and arrow, nor have I taken a flail. What is the problem in this that there should be some security arrangements here. (Yogacharya Anmol - You have demonic mind and poisonous tongue, what is the need of other weapons)

But your double standards keep aside the loved ones who have given you values for centuries. You save Your questions arise from me. I don't have any problem. From security arrangements because I do not believe that there is such a God as you believe. God is God, none is God. Godliness is an experience and I know that the soul does not die, but these security arrangements are not there to save the soul. But the body dies, the body is born and the body dies. And any thinking person can use his body as much as he wants. I want to do whatever I want with my body. There should be a complete system to save this body, no matter what. Those who love it will try to save it. I don't believe in stupid things. And you have asked are you God. Understand my meaning of saying God. I do not mean to say that I created this whole world. This kind of stupidity cannot be created in the world. I am not ready to take this responsibility. I will not accept this crime. And the fun is that you ask me, you did not ask Krishna, you did not ask Ram. That Ram created the world, could stop the sun and his wife was taken away by Ravana. Amazing Almighty. Big omnipresent, big omnipresent. Couldn't even save his wife and what will he save. He is universal, omnipotent, omnipresent and went to find the golden deer. A man who is more intelligent than a fool is worried whether there is a golden deer somewhere. But you will not ask him this question because you are sitting on this assumption. There is no question of asking. And then Sita was brought snatched from Lanka and her fire test was taken and this is universal. Since He is omnipresent, He is omnipresent, then he must know that Sita has not done any such work for which the fire test should be taken. What kind of universality is this? They don't even know this, they are worried that Sita might have become corrupt somewhere. This old Dakianusi husband's mind, that Sita's chastity may not be destroyed. Sita seems to be a more sensible woman. He didn't say come let's both get out of the fire together because you too stayed alone for so long. What is Krishna explaining in the entire Gita that fight, Arjun seems to be far more knowledgeable according to you. Because he is saying that what is the point in killing. The soul is immortal, now what to kill their bodies unnecessarily. Come on, I will meditate in the forest, I will meditate, there is no point in this. And the whole Gita of Krishna is organized for this thing that you fight. Got up Gandiv, Krishna does not know that the soul is not immortal. It is said that "Na Hanyate Na Hanyamane Sharire" the body dies, the soul does not die. But what did they mean by this? Because the soul does not die, there is no harm, therefore there is no violence. No one in the world has done as much violence as Krishna has done. Adolf Hitler, Genghis Khan, Nadirshah, Timurlang all fade away because They may have committed violence, but they do not have the support of violence, they know that they are doing wrong. Krishna made violence happen and gave it a complete philoshophical pomp. He explained to Arjuna that killing with carelessness because the soul does not die at all. Yes, what is the harm in killing them. These are earthen pots, break them and the soul will enter other houses. (Yogacharya Anmol - osho you change very quickly. If you are condemning the war, then you are very opportunistic, to make your point, you also praise the same war. You cry and to make your second point you also condemn the same war, full of cleverness) You consider all these people as God, and when I say that I am God, then you face difficulties. . And you don't even want to listen to my meaning, don't even want to understand. When I say that I am God, then I also say that you are also God. Godliness is our nature. It is another matter whether someone recognizes or does not recognize. The one who recognizes is God and the one who does not recognize is also God but he could not know. Some are asleep, some are awake. But the same consciousness resides within the one who is sleeping and awake. When I say that I am God, I do not say that I created the world. I am not even saying this as Krishna says whenever there is a loss of religion then I will come and protect it. First of all, when you came for the first time, which religion did you protect? Now what will the ashes protect? The truth is that the inhumanity of Krishna that happened at that time, it would be better if he does not come again. Please When we came, there was no protection, now what will we protect? I do not make any claim to protect religion. Nor do I claim that I am any Avatar. I do not like borrowed words. Why would I be an incarnation of Vishnu? Vishnu is not my avatar and I am not the avatar of Vishnu. I am not anyone's avatar, I have not come to protect anyone. I don't want to protect any religion, I don't want to save you from any sin. I am happy I know myself and I am happy. And it is a part of my pleasure that I should also introduce you to my pleasure. Then it is your pleasure, then whether you accept it or not, it is your property. And you say that you have a desire for worship. If I aspire for worship, you think I have some problem. I can get worship done everyday. I can offer flowers everyday. I can get the aarti performed everyday. What is the problem in this? Aarti of stones is being performed, so what is the problem in a living person in getting the Aarti performed. The picture that is stuck in my rosary is just to shock the Indian idiots and nothing else. (Yogacharya Anmol - See Indians are scoundrels in their eyes, who are you abusing, your parents are also Indians, you are making fun of the country and parents who brought you up by feeding and educating you.) is a joke and nothing else, but to understand the joke also a little intelligence is needed. Neither am I saying that someone should touch my feet. I am not asking anyone to worship me. Even if I come, I do not want anyone to stand up. Perhaps this will be the first religious meeting in India, in which the disciples of the Guru sit. (Yogacharya Anmol - You are sitting on the heights of foolishness, that's why you are asking such questions, if we stand in front of our teachers, then we do so to express our respect towards the teachers. Can't answer all the questions asked because I know my intelligence works only up to a limited range.I can't know all the incidents happening in this universe and same rule applies to every person in the world and in this You are also involved. That's why I will not question any pastimes done by God. My faith is not going to be shaken by your few questions. And what is the harm in it. Lord Ram and Lord Krishna give us a better way of life teaches us. By following them we will get benefit and not harm. You are asking all these questions out of jealousy, what harm can come to you from Ram and Lord Krishna who is so poisoned within you. Given by Lord Krishna The knowledge of Gita is changing people's lives. I am happy and the reason behind this happiness is my natural instinct. Knowledge of public style and Bhagwat Gita. Today I am propagating natural food style all over the world. Thousands of people from all over the world have been cured of many diseases by adopting this natural food style. Yes, with pure and natural food, not only the body but also the mind gets transformed. Today, if I have been able to provide selfless and free services to this common man, then I give the credit of this to Bhagwat Gita only. When I have achieved so much then why should I not have faith in Lord Krishna.) Have seen such gatherings where the Guru came and the disciple remained seated. This will probably be the first meeting where the Guru greets you with folded hands. What to worship, whose worship, but if you come with bounded beliefs, then there will be a hindrance. And if you come with bounded beliefs, then you will be deprived of the events that are happening here. A lot is happening here. Leave such small things Hansraj Vishnoi. Try to understand something, the temple is not being built here. Here there is no worshiper and no worshipper. Perhaps no one will return to the courtyard of the seasons. Come, live this guest with your life. Do you believe that tomorrow may or may not happen?

Comment by Yogacharya Anmol

First of all, I will appreciate the earlier lecture because in the first lecture some things have been said of the highest level which we should imbibe. And there are some reprehensible things in the same lecture which I will condemn. Because wrong must be called wrong and right must be called right.

Wow osho, what a logic you have given that if you want to progress then fight the war. War is not fought by looking at progress. War is fought for Dharma, war is fought against evil and not war is fought just for the sake of war because it will lead to progress. The war of Mahabharata was fought for the sake of religion, it was fought against evil, not because if the war of Mahabharata is fought then there will be progress. War is fought out of compulsion. When all options are exhausted, only war remains. That's why fighting a war becomes a compulsion because there is no option. No one fights war out of passion. Humanity can be protected by both war and peace. The first option should be peace. According to your logic, if progress is to be made then war should be fought. Suppose the one who fights the war will go ahead. So the one who stays behind will start a war. In this way one or the other will remain ahead and one or the other will remain behind and the war will go on continuously. That's why war is partially meaningful, not completely. We should live life with duty, we should fight with those who come in the way of duties. It seems that by reading more books and thinking more, some screws have loosened in your mind, on the contrary, direct lectures are being given.

osho's opportunism. osho was an opportunist. He used to present the facts in his own way to prove his point. I will put these facts before you, you have to decide.

Yes you must be thinking why I am saying this. What would you call a person who abuses Lord Krishna in one of his lectures and praises God in another of his lectures? In one lecture he praises the war of Mahabharata and in the second lecture he condemns the same war of Mahabharata. In one lecture, he praises the role of Lord Krishna in the war of Mahabharata and in another lecture, he puts him at par with Nadir Shah, Timur, Genghis Khan. What can be the similarity between Lord Krishna and Nadir Shah. The war of Mahabharata took place on two sides. There were soldiers on both sides. Both the sides had landed in the field of Kurukshetra with the desire of war. Both sides had weapons in their hands. It was a war of religion. There was a war between good and evil here. God had tried his best that there should be no war. But no matter how much you explain to a bad person, the matter of goodness does not enter his mind. A person who goes on committing heinous crimes, and does not understand even after explaining, has to take up arms. Not taking up arms in these circumstances would be impotence. And osho what do you want, attaining impotence by not fighting the war against evil. Do you want to create impotent in this society. To avoid war, God even asked Duryodhana to give only five villages. But that arrogant, sinful, heinous criminal who tried to disrobe a woman in full court, refused even this offer given by God. And you blame God for the war. You say that the decision Arjun was taking is correct. You say that Arjuna's decision to go to the forest and become a Yogi was right. How can it be meaningful if a person who has full potential to fight evil should run away by showing his back. You compare God with Nadir Shah, Nadir Shah had killed children, old people, women, unarmed people with swords. Were women and children attacked in the Kurukshetra war? Hey, we can't even call this a war, this is cowardice. And you are comparing Nadir Shah with God.

In one lecture you describe the war as meaningful and say that whatever Shri Krishna did was meaningful and in another lecture you condemn the same Kurukshetra war. And you put the blame on Lord Krishna. If this is not a sign of your being mentally ill then what is. If a person by his few words not only affects your mood but also creates an earthquake within you or in other words creates a volcano within you, then I have a question to you, are you your own master? Is. It seems to me that you are not your own master but your slave. Because if any person can change your mood by hitting a lump (stone) in your mind like a pond. Were you not able to progress even this much by walking on the yogic path. When you gave this lecture, the person asking the question was not even there (only followers of osho were present), so who were you listening to? Here it was not to narrate to anyone, but by making someone low, I had to establish myself high and pacify the flame that was burning inside.

osho read many books. Studied many philoshophers. it's a good thing. But did not know how to separate. Cooked khichdi after mixing all of them. There are many routes to reach a place. But we will choose only one path. Can't walk on many routes simultaneously. Let's take another example, if I want to go to the other side of the river, I will sit in only one boat and not in many. Although all the boats will go to that side only. But osho chose many routes at once, tried to sit on many boats at once. And that's why he got this mood. That's why he acquired a lot of knowledge but could not imbibe the knowledge.

osho, I heard people used to call you sex guru in the 60s. By the way, if it happens at that time then it is not a big deal because you have great interest in sex. You have written a whole book on sex. Wow, now you will get samadhi through sex. Whats up. All those who are of tamoguni and demonic nature must have become your followers. There must have been no dearth of followers. Because nowadays there is no dearth of people of demonic tendencies, Kalyug is still going on. Brother whatever you are, you are a number one artist gimmick. You are full of gimmicks. You have a lot of brain, that's why you have mastery in arguments. By the way, only people with brains do the work of fooling. By the way, there are some good qualities inside you too and seeing those qualities, if people with virtuous and good nature follow you then it is not surprising because there is some positivity inside you.

You say suppression is wrong and till now all the Vedas, Puranas and sages have shown suppression. While the reality is that they have taught to restrain the senses rather than suppression. There must be restraint on the senses because the senses do not have intelligence. That's why it cannot differentiate between good and bad. That's why senses should be curbed towards bad things, there is no suppression anywhere. Suppression means to suppress completely in every situation. osho has misrepresented the principles of Sanatana Dharma to establish his theory. osho was influenced by western civilization. He used to talk about Freud. But could not understand the basic ideas of Freud.

Writing this book of mine will be successful if you imbibe this one sentence said by me. You become the master of your mind, not a slave. Make yourself in such a way that no one can change your mood by throwing a stone in your mind like a pond. If this happens, then it should be understood that you are making good progress on the yogic path. Following this is also beneficial for the general public. If you are not able to do this, then this fight is not with anyone else but with yourself. Because you have to get the first victory over yourself.

In the end, I would like to say that I appreciate some things of the first lecture because that lecture is worthy of praise and condemn the second lecture. Because that lecture is worthy of condemnation. I leave it to you to decide whether osho was mentally ill or healthy. In fact, you gave the blasphemous lecture to pacify the volcano boiling inside you. As soon as a person asked you if you are God then show your powers, just like that your inner volcano erupted and for the next few days you kept burning inside and wrote this lecture with full strategy. And not only wrote, but spewed poison, which was building up inside you for so many days. You teach self-control to the world but you have no self-control. You don't have control over yourself. Only one question created turmoil within you. You don't even have that much sense, what kind of words should be used against the one in whom crores of people have faith. But what do you have to do with the faith of crores of people, you only had to pacify the volcano boiling inside you. Hey Osho, have you stooped so low that you thought only of yourself. No one can create waves in the mind of a Yogi, a self-controlled man. But here your mind was shaken by the questions of an ordinary person. A person is talking about yoga, whose own yoga has not happened. Perhaps you do not even know the meaning of Yoga and Yogi. And if we had known, we would have probably made some progress on this path. You only had knowledge of books, because you had read all the philoshophers of the world. But knowledge does not come just by reading books. Due to having more book knowledge, more and more people were affected. But you never got the knowledge of experience, because if you had, you would have become self-controlled.

osho is very clever, he quoted Lord Krishna to justify the war in the first lecture and did not even spare God to make his point in the lecture. See to what extent a person can stoop to fulfill his point of view.

Today it is the 20th day of writing this book and I am writing the answer to the last question given by osho. There are some words of wisdom in this discourse. Come on, it's good that I got something good, my time was not wasted. A question is arising in my mind whether I am making a mistake by writing this book. But then you get the answer if you learn something from osho's first lecture and imbibe the knowledge of one line written by me (Make your mind such that no one can create ripples in your mind like a pond by throwing a lump of stone in it. , as happened with osho) then this mistake is acceptable to me.

Discussion on Dr. Vikas Divyakirti

You must be wondering why I am discussing Divya Kirti ji in this book, actually osho had made the first hole in her mind. Now you have already come to know osho that what are his thoughts towards Lord Rama and Lord Krishna. Now he has filled the same thoughts in the mind of Dr. Vikas. The feeling that they have towards Lord Ram, Krishna is in front of you only. That's why it has become very important to discuss them as well.

Dibyakirti ji is an intelligent but emotionless person. He speaks after weighing his words. He knows the value of words. That's why he speaks neither a word less nor a word more. They know that if the words are kept correct and the sentiments are opposite why not, no one can raise a finger legally. But you have forgotten that communication is not only through words. Dialogue also happens with the feelings sitting inside us. Today's educated people have a problem, they accept only that thing which comes only in the realm of intellect. But don't forget that the scope of our intellect is limited and this creation is beyond the scope of intellect. But you don't want to go out of that range. I cannot say these things on the basis of your words, but those things are definitely visible in your feelings. And anyway, osho did the first hole in your mind. So that's why dew will definitely have an effect on you. And you can see what kind of opportunistic personality osho was that to prove his point (that I am right and all others are wrong) he calls the same person and events wrong as well as right. They are not saying the right thing because it is right, but because they have to prove their point right. He does not shy away from saying even that thing, after listening to which the hearts of crores of people got hurt.

My question is that no matter what that thing is the ultimate truth (even he does not know whether that thing is the ultimate truth or not, he only has an illusion that this is the ultimate truth, although I don't care about anyone's illusion As long as his delusion is not causing any harm to me. But if his delusion hurts my faith then I have a problem with his delusion) If the faith of crores of people gets hurt then how can it be right . The aim of all of us is to make everyone's life better. What good are you achieving by hurting people's faith. We don't have to learn from you which God to believe or not. Because even you do not know the ultimate truth. That's why Shri Krishna, Ram, Gautam Buddha, Mahavir are our Gods, we consider them as God and will continue to believe them.

I have a question to you whether writing anything in books makes it authentic. How many times do you give reference of some books that it is written like this in that book.

The kind of feelings you have towards Sanatan Dharma, Vedas and Lord Rama, and the way you develop unity in your mind towards God by reading the books written by a person like Purushottam Agarwal and being influenced by his books instead of reading Ramayana or Mahabharata. You are having a negative attitude. As Purushottam Agarwal has a background, he has received education from JNU, has been a professor in JNU itself and has been an ex-member of the Union Public Service Commission. Does its ideology which is in JNU and UPSC, the same ideology prevails here also. You are influenced by its ideology, it is clearly visible. Is there any agenda going on in JNU and UPSC towards Sanatan Dharma and Vedas? As Purushottam Agarwal picks up a verse from the Mahabharata and interprets it leaving out the context. It is foolish to extract its meaning from only one verse. Just like the way you say that people cut clips from my lectures or classes and put them on YouTube and it has a different meaning. Wow, you have a lot of mind, you have understood this very quickly, the meaning changes by cutting the clips, but why is it not understood that when only one verse is taken out from the whole book and presented, then its meaning Something else will also happen. But whoever has ill-will towards Sanatan Dharma and Lord Rama, will interpret it in such a way that the Vedas and the personality of Lord Rama can be degraded. Divyakirti, you are also no less opportunistic than osho, some other criteria for yourself and Mahabharata, and different criteria towards Ramayana and Lord Ram. Yes, you are very clever. By the way, Divya Kirti ji you have some good qualities and you are also spreading awareness on many subjects in the society. I also thank you for that.

Books cannot be trusted completely because the original texts can be tampered with. Adulteration can be done in this. But the truth of history cannot be changed by mere words. And that's why, despite so much adulteration, Lord Ram resides in the hearts of all of us. Do as much Adulteration as you want in the scriptures, our faith is not going to arise from Lord Rama, Lord Krishna and the Vedas. If you serve anything in writing in front of fools like you, you will accept everything as truth as if you read Purushottam Agarwal's book and accepted it as truth in that form. Without knowing what is the context of those verses. Now should I consider you an educated fool or a scholar. Now it should be known to the public that if a person occupies a high position, he can be a fool as well, not necessarily a scholar, as Purushottam Agarwal has already proved by writing that book. It is not necessary that if someone is sitting on the higher posts of UPSC, then he must be a scholar, he can be educated, he can be a fool, he can also be arrogant, who knows, after achieving such a high position, he will be filled with pride and consider himself Lord Ram and Started considering him higher than Lord Krishna and started finding faults in him. As osho and Purushottam did.

For the last one year, I have visited many religious places and by going there, I get the exact answer to my question that how India is one country despite so many diversities. The correct answer is our feelings. Our feelings are attached to Lord Rama and Krishna. He resides in the hearts of all of us. We may not know each other's language, but still we are connected to each other. I see that Southern India looks like a completely different country but when we see their customs, see temples, see God, we again connect with each other. Temples, deities, and our faith in Lord Ram, Lord Krishna have a big contribution in keeping the country united. It is because of faith that our feelings are connected to each other, due to which this country is also connected. But after getting 100-50 children admitted to IAS PCS, some institutes running Chutpunjee, their mind reaches the fourth sky and they start considering themselves above Lord Ram and Lord Krishna. Even after gaining so much intelligence, if you can't know that ego is bad, then what did you learn.

I am 35 years old. In my lifetime, I have learned the art of living life today. Under what circumstances, what decision has to be taken, it has been known. Decisions are very important. Because your decisions decide whether you will get sorrow or happiness in life. Most of the people's whole life ends but they do not know the art of living life. He can be a millionaire or even a billionaire. He can also be of sharp intellect. Even after all this, there is no guarantee that he has learned the art of living. Until you do not know this art, you will continue to suffer sorrows. Then your sharp intelligence and immense wealth are useless. And Bhagavad Gita teaches us that art. That's where I got this art. Food also plays an important role in knowing this art. That's why pay full attention to food as well. It is not easy to understand Bhagavad Gita. Before this I had studied in the year 2016 also but at that time this knowledge went out of my head. But in the year 2020, when I changed my diet due to my diseases and then after 8 to 10 months, when I started studying Bhagwat Gita again, the same verses seemed to me like diamonds and jewels. I used to meditate on each verse for five days. Only then could he imbibe the knowledge of that verse. I brought all those verses in my life. And today my Rome Rome is full of joy. It is very difficult to describe this joy in words. What is lacking in life. To get that thing, we start running behind that thing, it is a good thing that we must run. But we do not know how far to run. With knowledge you will be able to know that distance. You will know how much to collect. We go on hoarding like donkeys and life ends. And then we also say that there was great joy in childhood. Just lack of knowledge, your childhood will come even today. Actually you have not been able to know the importance of things. Haven't been able to know who has to give how much time. We have given all the importance to only one thing. But life is a game of balance. I am 35 and for the last three years I am happier than my childhood. And all this is achieved only by pure food and divine knowledge. Make this change in your life and you too will become happy.

Statement of Yogacharya Anmol

In the end, I would say that we all are a part of the same God, our soul is a part of the same God and we have taken this gross body from this earth, the earth which is integral is only one. In this way we are all the same, there is no difference. Conflict occurs when there are two different things. When there is no difference then there is no conflict. That's why there is no difference between you and me O O O O Dibyakirti. We are one. That's why I have no hatred towards you. I have no hatred towards you. If wrong is not called wrong, then how will the person who commits the mistake know what mistake he is doing. That's why don't just dismiss my statements with ego, whether you accept my statements or not, but do introspect. osho is no more so this message is for the followers of osho. osho has good qualities as well as bad qualities, so I have no problem in accepting their good qualities. And will be ahead in calling bad things bad, because if you don't say bad things bad, then how will the person saying bad things know that he has said something bad. Divya Kirti ji is also doing better work, and can contribute better, but he should take care of people's beliefs.

Thank You with love

Yogacharya Shri Anmol Yadav

www.ingramcontent.com/pod-product-compliance
Lightning Source LLC
Chambersburg PA
CBHW030413160726
47992CB00007B/3103